Judaism
In Plain and Simple English

BookCaps™ Study Guides
www.bookcaps.com

© 2012. All Rights Reserved.

Table of Contents

INTRODUCTION 4

CHAPTER 1: HISTORY 5
- Introduction 5
- Origins 5
- Antiquity 5
- Persecutions 5
- Hasidism 5
- The Enlightenment and new religious movements 5
- Spectrum of observance 5

CHAPTER 2: PRINCIPLES OF FAITH 5
- Core Tenets 5

CHAPTER 3: JEWISH RELIGIOUS TEXTS 5
- Jewish legal literature 5
- The Written Torah 5
- Scrolls 5
- The Oral Torah 5
- Other Important Jewish Writings 5
- Jewish Philosophy 5
- Rabbinic Hermeneutics 5

CHAPTER 4: JEWISH OBSERVATIONS 5
- Jewish ethics 5
- Prayers 5
- Religious clothing 5
- Torah readings 5
- Synagogues and religious buildings 5
- Dietary laws: kashrut 5
- Laws of ritual purity 5
- Family Purity 5
- Life-cycle events 5

CHAPTER 5: JEWISH HOLIDAYS 5
- Shabbat 5
- Three pilgrimage festivals 5
- High holy days 5

  PURIM 5
  HANUKKAH 5
  OTHER HOLIDAYS 5
CHAPTER 6: OTHER RELIGION 5
  INFLUENCE ON CHRISTIANITY 5
  INFLUENCE ON ISLAM 5
CONCLUSION 5
ABOUT THE PUBLISHER 5

Introduction

Did you ever hear the one about the Jewish telegram that simply read: 'Start worrying. Details to follow'?

Like the one above, there are plenty of stereotypes that exist about Judaism. One thing, though, is for certain. This is a really interesting religion that has been around for thousands of years, and it has an enthralling history. Sometimes that history has been sad, but it's an enduring religion that is still followed by plenty of people today.

Woody Allen, Albert Einstein, Mel Brooks, Leonard Bernstein, Natalie Portman and Elizabeth Taylor are all Jewish, and who doesn't like the work they do? (They're not the only Jews; they're just some famous ones we found to get you interested. There are actually more than 13.1 million Jews around today.)

So, with that in mind, let's take a look at Judaism and some of the key figures from the religion's history.

Chapter 1: History

Introduction

From Abraham to Anne Frank and beyond, the history of Judaism is filled with interesting people and some great stories. After all, who could fail to raise a smile at the idea of Abraham discovering monotheism and then having something of a strop and smashing up all his father's idols? Sometimes the history of religion can seem a bit odd from a modern standpoint, but it provides an interesting insight into how Judaism first came about. Plus, the religion started more than 3500 years ago, so there's bound to be a whole lot of variety in there! Let's find out more...

Origins

So, Judaism has been around for thousands of years, which means that it began in the Bronze Age. Specifically, it began in the Middle East with a nomad called Abram, who we now know as Abraham. If he was around today, he'd probably be pretty chuffed that he's come to be known as the first Patriarch of the Jews. He was told by God that he'd become the leader of a great people if he did as He said (which makes God sound a bit like a parent telling their child 'if you want your dessert, you have to eat your vegetables', but we guess that's His prerogative). Abraham is important because he was the one who pioneered the idea that there's only one God.

You can read the story of Abraham in Genesis, the first book of the bible. He was from Mesopotamia, which today we call Iraq. His father made a living selling idols of gods; there are stories of how Abraham smashed up those idols when he came to his realisation that there is only one God. This is said to be the birth of monotheism.

God certainly put Abraham through his paces, testing his faith to the limit. Think of it like a marathon: you'll get great rewards at the end, but, along the way, there are times when you probably just want to curl up in a ball at the side of the road and have a bit of a cry. For instance, God made Abraham move with his wife Sarah, promising him land, descendants and a relationship with God. This move is why the name 'Abram' was changed to 'Abraham': God rewarded Abraham by giving him a name that means 'Father of the people'.

There were more tests along the way, too, notably God asking Abraham to sacrifice his son Isaac, only to spare his life at the last moment. In a way, we can see echoes of the relationship between God and Abraham today. We often do things for people in exchange for them doing something for us: that is exactly what God and Abraham were doing too. God wanted Abraham's faith in order to create a value-led religion; in return, God kept his promises to Abraham.

Abraham's son Isaac, who was spared from sacrifice at the last moment, is the second of three patriarchs of Judaism. His wife Rebecca gave birth to twins called Esau and Jacob. The twin boys did not get on and there are many stories of how they were at war with each other before they were even born – we may worry about sibling rivalry today, but when a new religion is starting to evolve, you can imagine how serious the tension was between these two boys!

Eventually, after Jacob received a blessing that was meant for Esau, Jacob went to live with his uncle. He ended up marrying four women: Leah, Rachel and their maids, Zilphah and Bilhah. He had one daughter and 12 sons. Jacob is particularly significant in Judaism because one day, he went back to his homeland with the intention of making peace with his brother. On the way, he ended up wrestling with a man who was eventually revealed to be an angel. The angel called Jacob 'Israel', which means 'the Champion of God'.

This is why Jewish people are often referred to as the Children of Israel: this relates to the fact they descended from Jacob. His sons became the fathers of the tribes of Israel. Over time, his descendants ended up becoming enslaved in Egypt. This situation was only rectified when Moses was tasked with getting all of the Jews out of Egypt – like a sort of mass prison break, with massively high stakes. Luckily, he succeeded.

The Jews followed Moses as God led them to a place called Mount Sinai, crossing the Red Sea to get there. This is one of the most famous events in Jewish history, where God revealed himself to the people, and they became a nation. He told them that if they observed his rules, they would become a 'holy nation'. The nation of the Children of Israel agreed to do everything that God had asked of them, and it is said that every single Jewish soul that will ever be born was there at Mount Sinai, ready to be bound to what God had asked of them (must've been crowded!).

He later gave to Moses the Ten Commandments – Moses spent 40 days at the mountain, listening as God handed down the commandments to him and told him how to apply them (this is called the Oral Law). Over the next 40 years, the Written Law of the Jewish people was established in the Torah. These are the books of the bible called Genesis, Exodus, Leviticus, Numbers and Deuteronomy. Collectively they are often known as the Books of Moses, to represent the special part Moses played in the origins of Judaism.

Antiquity

Now we come to the antiquity period – what we could call a honeymoon period of Judaism. This followed the Exodus from Egypt but came before splits started to appear. The period is usually called the United Monarchy.

The United Monarchy came about because the tribes of Israel experienced Philistine aggression: the Philistines were better equipped than the Jewish people and there was a worry that their independence could come under threat. This, coupled with the fact that other powers such as Egypt, Babylon and Assyria were too weak to influence anything at the time, inspired the Israelites to come closer together. This led to the establishment of the monarchy under the leadership of Saul.

However, Saul wasn't entirely successful in his task and so it was left to his successor David to consolidate the kingdom and expand Israel. The city of Jerusalem was the capital city, and he established the Davidec Empire. Solomon's rule followed David's; he is said to have presided over the Golden Age of Israel. He undertook huge building and development projects and extended Israel's international links through marriage – but he was something of what we might call a Big Spender.

After the rule of Solomon, the state of Israel was split into two separate kingdoms. The Kingdom of Israel remained in the north, while the Kingdom of Judah was in the south. The split occurred because Solomon had been too extravagant; land was taken to pay for this (imagine having the bailiffs called in on a country!) and upon his death, the people in the north refused to recognise the leadership of his son. Jerusalem became the capital of Judah, and Samaria was the capital of Israel.

This division stayed in place for 200 years. During that time, the Kingdoms decreased in power and size. This was a problem due to the fact there were major powers located close to both Israel and Judah. Israel was conquered by the Assyrians in 722BC, and the tribes that made up Israel were scattered across the Assyrian Empire; they were never to be heard from again. Later on, the Babylonians conquered Judah, but when the Judean Jews were relocated, this happened in a single block, in effect creating the first Jewish diaspora.

Eventually, though, the Persians conquered the Babylonians and this allowed the Judeans to return to their homeland. This was not without tension and trouble within itself: a great deal went on in international relations before the Babylonians suffered a defeat. Over the years, Judah became a tribute state to Egypt and later to Babylon – they must've been fed up of getting passed from superpower to superpower! At one point, the king of Judah defected to Egypt, which provoked a backlash amongst the Babylonians. Around 10,000 Jews ended up getting deported to Babylon. This was the start of what is known as the Exile.

This was essentially the end of the Jewish kingdom and for many Jews, particularly those who were left homeless in Babylon. It seemed as though God had broken his promise to give the people their own nation. The original glory of the kingdom started by David had gone, and the religion of Judaism was at something of a crossroads.

Historical Jewish groupings (to 1700)
Imagine you are in a room with a few million other people. Okay, maybe not a room. Maybe a very big field. Now, do you reckon all of you would think exactly the same about things? Chances are that you wouldn't. With this in mind, it's easy to see why Jewish people don't all think the same, either. Of course, throughout history they have all had enough in common to keep the religion together, but just as with any other group of humans, they've also had enough disagreements to split into different factions.

We can see this sort of thing today in political coalitions: coalition governments are often formed on the basis of what they agree on, but they often end up splitting up again because they disagree on other, fundamental issues. This was the sort of thing that happened to Judaism following the antiquity period. For example, Christianity broke off to become its own religion.

Other groups of Jews of note include the Pharisees, Sadducees, Essenes, Herodians and Zealots. While they were all very influential at the time, most of their influence had begun to wane by 1CE. However, the Pharisees survived in the form of Rabbinic Judaism and ended up developing the belief system that most Jews live by today, making it one of the most enduring strands of the religious tradition. One of the main reasons the Rabbinic Jews were able to survive was because, following the imposition of Roman rule, they were able to adapt to represent both the Jews and the Romans (cunning!).

This allowed for the survival of Judaism, and as the centuries progressed, Jewish people started to settle in an increasing number of countries. This had the effect of creating more distinct historical Jewish groupings. For example, the Sephardic Jews are typically found in Spain, Portugal, North Africa and the Middle East. These are split into Sephardic in Spain and Portugal and Midrashim in the Middle East and Africa.

The fact that these two tenets of Judaism have so much in common despite being in different locations meant that when the Jews were exiled from Spain in the 15th century, they were largely able to find homes in Midrashim communities. When North America began to be colonised, the majority of the early Jewish settlers were Sephardic and evidence of their living there can be traced back to 1684.

However, in time more Ashkenazi Jews ended up living in North America. This is a type of Judaism that is typically associated with Eastern Europe, Germany and France and the word 'Ashkenaz' refers to Germany. Ashkenazi Jews are historically less likely to integrate with other, non-Jewish communities. For instance, where Ashkenazi Jews lived close by to Christians, there were typically more tensions than in areas where the Midrashim Jews lived in Muslim-controlled regions.

This reminds us a bit of living in an area with two competing football teams – no matter how much you like your neighbours for their other traits, it can be hard to get past the all-important fact that they don't support the same team as you.

Other smaller groups of Jewish people developed, too. These include Ethiopian Jews, Asian Jews and Yemenite Jews, but these were typically smaller in number although they still exist today, along with the Ashkenazi and Sephardic/Midrashim groups.

Persecutions

Now we move on to something of a sobering topic: persecution. We've all heard the story of the Holocaust and the personal story of Anne Frank, right? They're devastatingly sad, and, unfortunately, there are loads of other instances of persecution throughout history.

Sometimes this has been due to a religious motive; at other times, it has been political. For example, in 70CE, the Roman Army killed more than 1 million Jews and destroyed the city of Jerusalem. In 115-117, Jews revolted against the Roman Empire, leading to hundreds of thousands of deaths. In 135, the Romans seriously restricted the Jews' freedom to worship and in 200, people were banned from converting to Judaism.

Much of the historical persecution of Jewish people has been perpetrated by Christians. For example, in 306CE, marriages between Jews and Christians were banned by the Synod of Elvira. The 315CE Edict of Milan caused Jews to lose lots of rights, including the right to live in Jerusalem. Over time, synagogues were burned, Jews were forced to flee cities such as Alexandria in Egypt, and even respected philosophers such as St. Augustine wrote against the Jews.

In Spain in 613BC, Jewish children were taken from their parents and then given a Christian education. Jewish people were told to convert their religion or leave the country. In 722CE, Pope Leo III outlawed Judaism and forced Jews to be baptised. By the time the first Crusade started, in 1096, even though the main aim of the crusade was to liberate Jerusalem, many Jews were killed along the way – this was a theme that was to raise its head again throughout subsequent Crusades.

Jews were persecuted in many countries, including Spain, Italy, England and Flanders (modern-day Belgium). This included their houses being burned, their possessions being seized by the state, being forced to convert or made to go somewhere else. Austria, Bavaria, France and Portugal also persecuted Jews hundreds of years ago.

In 1306, France exiled 100,000 Jews with nothing but the clothes on their backs and enough food to last them for a day. In 1321, 5000 Jews were burned at the stake in France. When the Black Death began to grip Europe in the 1300s, it was noted that fewer Jews than Christians were dying, largely due to their sanitary rules. This led many Christians to believe that the Jews were being protected by Satan. Many of them died of torture rather than the Black Death.

One notable persecution of the Jews took place in 1516, when the Governor of the Republic of Venice created the first ghetto in Europe, ordering the Jews to live there. Over the next few hundred years, many countries across Europe continued to take action against the Jews. This was largely due to Christian teachings that the Jews were responsible for the death of Jesus. However, with a few exceptions, they largely kept them alive despite making their lives a misery, as it was thought the Jews had a role to play in the 'end times'.

From 1800 onwards, the persecution of the Jews continued, and the term 'anti-Semitism' was invented in 1873. In 1915, Russia forcibly moved 600,000 Jews, about 100,000 of whom died. 200,000 Jews were murdered in Ukraine in 1917, and in 1925, Hitler wrote *Mein Kampf,* promoting hatred of the Jewish people. This eventually led to the mass slaughter of millions of Jews in that awful event of the Second World War: the Holocaust.

Arguably, since WW2, the persecution of the Jews has lessened, but it still continues until this day, proving not only the brutality that humans can inflict on each other but also the resilience of this religion and its people.

Hasidism

Ever felt that there was something missing but not been quite sure what it is? This is the sort of feeling that led to the creation of the Hasidic Jewish movement. It began in the 1700s, in Eastern Europe, and was founded by Rabbi Israel Baal Shem Tov. He is often referred to as Besht, which is a shortening of his name. He was well-known as a scholar and he was committed to studying both the inner and outer workings of the Torah.

Besht developed a strand of Judaism that is highly dedicated to the teachings of the Torah. It is also heavily focused on developing the relationship of Jewish people with God. The idea behind this is helping Jews to feel closer to God with everything they do.

This is where the difference between the Hasidic movement and other forms of Judaism lay: one of the concerns many Jewish people had with their religion at the time was that it was too academic, and the leaders were focused too much on the intellectual aspects of practicing Judaism (like school science teachers going on about theory when all you want to do is have a go with the Bunsen burner). By contrast, Hasidism was based around developing a good connection with God and the Torah.

It didn't take too long before differences began to rear up between Hasidic Jews and those following non-Hasidic paths. It was felt by some Jews who didn't follow Hasidism that the Hasidic form of worship was too exuberant, and they also disagreed with the fact that Hasidic Jews were changing the times they prayed – something that many felt was wrong. However – and luckily – most of these differences were relatively short-lived and within a couple of generations the majority of the rifts between the two groups had healed.

Over time, Hasidism actually came to inform non-Hasidic branches of Judaism. Non-Hasidic practices have also had a tempering effect on some of the more extreme practices of the Hasidic Jews. The rift between the groups still exists, though, and it is particularly evident in modern day Israel.

Hasidism is a form of Jewish Orthodoxy. However, it is distinct from other forms of Orthodoxy due to their devotion to the study of the Torah and the fact Hasidic Jews tend to wear very distinctive clothes. They are also devoted to a dynastic leader, and there are around 12 big Hasidic Jewish movements still around today.

Over the centuries, Hasidism has made its way across Europe and into North America. Fairly soon after the practice was first established, Hasidic sects were founded right across Europe. Mass immigration to North America in the late 19th century meant it found its way across the Atlantic, too.

Today, the largest Hasidic movement is the Lubavitch group. They have their headquarters in Brooklyn in New York and that movement alone has got around 100,000 followers. Many people in Israel follow this movement, but other Hasidic movements are also prominent in Israel.

> Interesting Fact: Woody Allen is from an Orthodox family who lived in a Hasidic area in Brooklyn.

The Enlightenment and new religious movements

The 18th century brought on great developments in European thinking. This period came to be known as the Enlightenment, and it was characterised by a focus on human reason, and the idea that this could be used as a catalyst to create a better world. This was positive for the Jews in some ways as European thinkers started to argue in their favour and many governments relaxed their persecution of the Jews, although this was not true of everywhere.

However, alongside the European Enlightenment came the Jewish Enlightenment. Jews were helped to integrate into secular societies, meaning that they were able to receive more opportunities, particularly in terms of education. They were encouraged to integrate further into European communities and learn the relevant languages, while still maintaining their commitment to and knowledge of Hebrew.

One of the main aims of this was to try and improve the typically tense relations between Jews and Christians. There was also a strong, understandable desire among Jewish communities to improve their legal position and gain more rights for themselves. A man named Moses Mendelssohn was responsible for leading much of this movement on behalf of the Jewish people. He wanted Judaism to be seen as open to change and as part of the move towards enlightened, rational thinking.

The wider Enlightenment led to other changes such as the French Revolution, following which legal emancipation was granted to Jews in France. They agreed to see themselves as a religious group and pledged allegiance to the French state. This raised a new dichotomy: gaining legal recognition and acceptance for their religion, but at the same time losing part of their identity by accepting another nationality. Think of it a bit like a diet – you really want the svelte figure dieting will give you, but giving up cake to get it really hurts. It might be a totally different situation, but the concept of a trade-off is very familiar to Jews.

The Enlightenment also helped to bring about the Industrial Revolution in Western Europe, and the Jews had an important part to play in this. Many of them entered important professions such as banking, the law and science, with great success as entrepreneurs. While this was in many ways positive for Judaism, it also increased hostility towards the Jews in other ways due to their success in business.

This hostility was particularly felt in Germany and, as a result, many German Jews emigrated to America. However, Western European Jews had gained legal equality by the end of the 1800s. Switzerland (1874) and Spain (1918) were the last two countries to do this.

Another effect of the Enlightenment was that it encouraged the development of new forms of Judaism. Notable among these was Reform Judaism, which started in Germany but really took hold in Britain in 1842. The aim of Reform Judaism is to embrace the modernity that came with the Enlightenment while still holding onto many of the traditional Jewish practices. However, in reaction to this, the Modern Orthodox movement was created.

Modern Orthodoxy is fairly strict in terms of following traditions unlike some other forms of Judaism in the wake of the Enlightenment. It allows for exposure to modern and secular ideas, but is very keen on keeping to Jewish customs. From these new forms of Judaism, alliances such as the Conservative movement were formed.

Spectrum of observance

Let's take a look at some interesting facts about Jewish worship to find out more about the spectrum of observance – essentially, this refers to religious statistics, such as how many Jews worship in a particular way.

In the twenty first century, Jewish populations are found in countries all over the world. As you might expect, Israel has got the largest number of Jews out of all countries, with Jewish people making up an estimated 42.5% of the world's Jewish population. The United States of America contributes 39.3% of the world's Jewish population and France 3.6%. Canada is estimated to have 2.8% of the world's Jewish people and the United Kingdom has 2.2%.

Other countries with significant Jewish populations include Russia, Argentina, Germany, Australia and Brazil. As you might expect with such a diverse religion made up of people living in countries all over the world, there is great variety in the spectrum of observance and how much time Jewish people spend on religious activities.

For example, in Brazil the Jewish population draws on both Sephardi and Ashkenazi influences. It also contains both liberal and orthodox Jews, and so there is quite a wide spectrum of observance even though Brazil accounts for only a small percentage of the world's Jewish population.

Also, in Israel there has been speculation in the past that only around 20% of the Jewish population are seriously religious, with most people actually being fairly secular but coerced into worship by their more passionate peers. However, statistics suggest that the country is actually more religious than many might think; while there are definitely secular Jewish elements in Israel just as there are in every other country, observance of the religion is actually very important.

It is particularly interesting to look at the state of Israel, as this is the historic home of the Jews and also contains the largest population. One study found that 56% of the population always light Shabbat candles, with 22% doing this sometimes and only 20% never doing it at all, suggesting there is a significant following for this particular Jewish tradition.

However, the same study found that 56% of the population never went to synagogue, which suggests that many Jewish people are choosing to worship in their own way and observing the traditions that are suitable to them; 70% fast on Yom Kippur and 78% participate in Passover Seder. This shows that religious worship is important to people in Israel, but this doesn't necessarily have to take place in a church.

These trends can be seen replicated in the USA, where we find the world's second largest Jewish population. For example, out of upwards of 5 million Jews, more than 4.3 million have a connection with the religion. However, only 48% belong to a synagogue with even fewer attending services on a regular basis, again suggesting that religion for Jewish people is not just found in places of worship.

In the United Kingdom, around 1 in 6 British Jews are attached to Reform Judaism. Others belong to Conservative movements, which are often known as Masorti Judaism in the UK. There are around 30 Liberal Judaism synagogues in the UK and many British Jews belong to the Orthodox tradition, again showing the diversity within the religion even within a single country.

Chapter 2: Principles of Faith

Core Tenets

We've taken a good look at the history of Judaism, but what do they actually believe? All religions have rules to live by and Judaism is no exception.

Another way to think of this is how parents often lay down a set of house rules for their children to abide by – but those rules aren't always entirely obeyed and there is often debate as to their virtue and relevance among some members of the family.

This is a tussle that can easily be related to the core tenets of Judaism, which have been contested and debated over the centuries since the religion was first established. You may have heard of the 13 Principles of Faith, which is the most popular formation of what Jewish people believe. These Principles were developed by Rabbi Moshe ben Maimon, who is otherwise known as the Rambam.

He took the Torah, the Jewish holy book, as his inspiration in creating these 13 Principles of Faith. He called them 'the fundamental truths of our religion and its very foundations.' There are different ways of writing out the 13 Principles, but below is one interpretation to give you an idea of what they entail and what Jewish people believe: many Jewish congregations recite a more poetic form of the Principles in the synagogue every day after their prayers, including the words *Ani Maamin*, which means 'I believe'.

1) God exists and is the reason that everything else exists
2) God is unique
3) God is incorporeal, meaning he is not affected by physical experiences
4) God is eternal; he existed before anything else and he will exist after all else has gone
5) Jewish people can pray to only one God; praying to other or false gods is not allowed
6) God speaks to Man through prophecy; the word of the prophet must be believed
7) Moses is the greatest prophet of them all
8) God gave the Oral and Written Torah to Moses
9) The Torah should not be replaced, or anything else used in its place
10) God is omniscient, meaning He knows what men do and think
11) There is divine retribution; God punishes the evil and rewards the good – he knows who is

good and who is evil so that He can act accordingly when the time comes
12) The Messiah and the messianic era will come, but people who aim to calculate the arrival of this era have little wisdom
13) The dead can be resurrected

As we have already seen in previous sections, Judaism is a very diverse religion and so even though many Jews subscribe to all of the above 13 Principles of Faith, they are also contested by many others. In particular, the more liberal forms of Judaism tend to take issue with some if not most of the Principles.

One of the reasons the Principles aren't always strictly adhered to is because there is no formal set of beliefs that Jewish people are required to believe in. This is because Judaism is more about action than belief and, while belief undoubtedly plays a huge role in the religion, it is not the only important aspect of it. However, one thing the vast majority of Jews agree on is that Judaism is all about the relationship between God, Israel and Man; it is how this relationship should play out that causes disagreements to occur.

Also, when you consider that Rambam developed his list of Principles in the 12th century, it makes sense that they are somewhat disputed today. After all, the world has changed a lot, particularly since the Enlightenment, and even though the roots of the religion are the same, Judaism has also changed, and new branches of it have developed. The Principles were criticised even when they were first developed, though. Many of the criticisms stem from the fact that even though everything written in the Principles is true, not all of it is fundamental to the Jewish faith.

Interesting Fact: Rambam is called Rambam because it's an acrostic of his full name: Rabbi Moshe ben Maimon.

However, some say that this is where much of the strength of Judaism lies: the fact that there is no formal set of beliefs, and there are different interpretations of the Principles means there is room for personal opinion and different varieties of Judaism to grow, as well.

For example, as mentioned above, Judaism is focused on the triad of God, mankind and Israel. This is written about in the Jewish scriptures, which also discuss some of the obligations involved in these relationships. But what are these obligations? Essentially, they are the commandments set out in the Torah and given by God. The obligations also include long-standing customs of the Jewish faith and some laws set out by influential rabbis. These obligations refer to the action of Judaism rather than tenets of belief.

Different branches of Judaism see these obligations differently. For instance, Orthodox Jews tend to believe that these obligations are absolute and unchanging no matter how much the rest of the world changes. Conservative Jews believe that these rules of God evolve over time. Reconstructionist and Reform movements of Judaism tend to believe that the obligations talked about in the scriptures are more like guidelines and that people can choose whether they are going to follow them.

From this, we can see that even though Jewish people have much in common when it comes to the core tenets and Principles of Faith, these are not set in stone. This reflects the nature of the religion and the way that it has evolved over the centuries.

However, despite the conflict and different interpretations of the matter, the Principles of Faith are still vital to the core tenets of Judaism and their importance in helping us understand what Jewish people believe and what guides them in their religion cannot be underestimated. Different movements of Judaism might alter how they see the Principles according to their own beliefs but, having been around for almost a millennium already, it seems safe to say the Principles will not be going anywhere any time soon.

Chapter 3: Jewish Religious Texts

Jewish legal literature

Calling it 'legal literature' admittedly takes some of the fun out of it, but this is a really important aspect of Judaism. In particular, we are talking about the Torah.

We have already seen in previous sections that the Written Torah is made up of the first five books of the bible, which are also often known as the Five Books of Moses. This is also known as Chameesha Choomshey Torah in Hebrew.

However, just as with many other aspects of Judaism, there are different interpretations for the word 'Torah'. The above explanation, concerning the Five Books of Moses, is the most limited. 'Torah' can also refer to the entire Written Torah, which is known as the Old Testament to people who are not Jewish. The most encompassing explanation of 'Torah' is the one that includes all Jewish teachings.

It's no wonder people get so confused sometimes!

The Written Torah

In other words, the Written Torah is the 'Old Testament' to Christians and other people who do not follow Judaism. Jewish people sometimes also call the Written Torah the Tanakh. This is split into three different sections, each of which covers different aspects of Jewish law and tradition.

- The Torah, which consists of the first five books of the bible and makes up Jewish Law.
- The Nevi'im, which means the 'Prophets'. This takes through from Joshua to Malakhi.
- The Kevuthim, which means the 'Writings'. This includes the books from Psalms to Chronicles.

All of the books included in the Written Torah have Hebrew translations, but for the purposes of this explanation, we are sticking to the more familiar English names. Many of the Hebrew translations are similar or even the same as the English names, but it is important to note that there are some differences to found, as well.

> Interesting Fact: The reason the Written Torah is sometimes called the Tanakh is because 'Tanakh' is an acrostic of Torah, Nevi'im and Kevuthim.

Scrolls

The Written Torah forms an important part of Jewish services at the synagogue, and sermons are popularly written on scrolls of parchment. This usually takes place on a Monday and Thursday, when small sections of the hand-written scrolls are read, and on the Shabbat, which is when the main reading occurs. The scrolls are always read in sequence, and it usually takes a year for the entire scroll to be read out. That's some dedication.

Reading the Torah scrolls is a valuable skill because they are written in a special way, without using any vowels. Also, the reading is not usually spoken: instead, it is sung. This means the person in charge of the reading generally has to be very knowledgeable about the scriptures or else there is a high chance they could make a mistake. We imagine they'd also have to be pretty confident about singing in public!

> Interesting Fact: It can take up to 18 months for a scroll to be created. This is because the animal skin used to make the parchment has to be prepared properly before the scriptures are written out by hand; even a single mistake can mean the process has to be begun again.

The Oral Torah

The purpose of the Oral Torah, otherwise known as the Talmud, is to provide guidance in terms of how to apply the Written Torah and what the laws laid out in this actually mean. It is widely believed among Jews, particularly those who follow the Orthodox tradition, that the Oral Torah was imparted to Moses by God. It was then taught to others so that the tradition is still alive today.

However, even though the Oral Torah was originally in spoken form only, by around the second century, all of the oral teachings were compiled and written up in a document that is known as the Mishnah. As time passed, more information was added to the Mishnah, included additions that came from Babylon and Jerusalem. These additions are called the Gemara. Together they make up the Talmud.

> Interesting Fact: There are two Talmuds. The more comprehensive Babylonian Talmud and the one that is referred to most often as simply the Talmud, and the Jerusalem Talmud.

Many people find the Talmud quite difficult to read because of the way it is written. One way of thinking of this is reading about an event you are vaguely aware of but don't know much about, or reading someone else's report of a class field trip that you didn't go on (even though you probably should have, oops) – you are at least somewhat aware of the context and what the aim is, but as you are one step removed, it can be confusing. The Talmud requires a certain amount of prior knowledge, which means if you are not already informed, it's easy to get lost – like if someone talks about a TV show that you've seen but are a couple of seasons behind on.

Another reason many people find the Talmud difficult to comprehend is that it often provides several interpretations for each issue without making it clear which interpretation is the preferred option – like when your parents give you conflicting instructions, but then completely fail to come to an agreement as to which you should go along with.

The Talmud discusses a wide range of issues related to Jewish laws and tradition. These include:
- Agricultural issues and laws
- Festivals, in particular the Shabbat
- Marriage and divorce
- Financial laws, including tort laws
- The Temple and issues relating to sacrifices
- Purity and impurity

> Interesting Fact: Many Jews have a commitment to study one page of the Talmud every day. It can take around seven and a half years to complete a single cycle.

Other Important Jewish Writings

While the Written Torah and Oral Torah make up the most important aspects of Jewish laws and tradition, there are other writings that it is worth taking note of. In particular, there are many stories that embellish on certain aspects of the Torah, such as stories in the bible. These provide a greater level of background and detail to give people more information about the religion.

A good example of this is the story of Abraham discovering there is only one God. We have discussed earlier in this guide of the stories detailing him smashing up his father's idols; this particular story involves him smashing up all of the idols with the exception of the largest one. When his father discovered the mess, Abraham blamed the largest idol for what had happened – this is generally seen as a way of demonstrating the fact that the multiple idols had no power and the only power resides in monotheism.

We reckon it's also a good distraction for a child trying to avoid a parental telling off. It's something that's pretty familiar to people today, too. See familiar excuses such as 'the dog ate my homework' and 'I didn't break the vase, the baby did.'

As well as the stories, which are known as Midrashim, there are also a lot of responses to questions raised by Jewish law. These are generally written by wise rabbis who have been questioned about difficult issues; they review and interpret the Torah in the light of the questions and come up with an argument for their interpretation. Eventually, many of these interpretations were collected into written volumes. As time has progressed, the interpretations have come to include topics such as cosmetic surgery and dishwashers, as well as traditional Jewish issues.

All of this goes to show just how much there is to say about Jewish law and how many interpretations have been created for it. However, many new interpretations come to light, though, the Oral and Written Torah will always be there, forming the basis of the law.

Jewish Philosophy

The idea of Jewish philosophy is not about drunken conversations in a bar as it is for most of the rest of us. Instead, it's all about inquiry based on the holy texts, traditions and wider experiences of the Jewish people. It covers everything from political debate to ponderings on the nature of the universe. What distinguishes Jewish philosophy from other forms of philosophy is that it believes Jewish teachings have something important to say about the world and the nature of life.

Being a good Jewish philosopher generally means being able to speak several different languages and being willing to listen to a wide range of conflicting views in order to understand people's viewpoints. It is all about discovering what is relevant within Judaism today: the practice of philosophy is always evolving, and it is about what is happening now and theories of the future as well as traditions and what has gone on in the past.

Jewish philosophy is concerned with lots of different things, including:
- The relationship between God and the Jewish people
- The meaning of the mission of Judaism
- The laws, rituals and customs of Judaism
- How these rituals relate to the rest of humanity
- Zionism

- The holocaust and other examples of persecution
- Jewish diasporas
- The creation and development of the Jewish experience
- Different movements of Judaism
- Jewish humour

This is not a full list of what is considered in Jewish philosophy as it can, simply, involve the study of practically anything. Some Jewish philosophers are quite broad in the subjects they study while others specialise in topics of interest to them. For example, Pico della Mirandola looked at Kabbalah, Buber was interested in Hasidism, and Freud was interested in humour, among other things.

There are a couple of weaknesses that are often attributed to modern Jewish philosophy, namely a tendency to be too historical in its approach and a tendency to be too narrow in terms of what it looks at. One of its strengths, however, is that it is distinctly Jewish: the fact that Jewish philosophers have access to so many Hebrew sources and other interesting information means they have a unique outlook that sets them apart from other strands of philosophy.

There are lots of notable Jewish philosophers from throughout history who have made important contributions to the tradition. For example, Philo of Alexandria is generally considered to have had very important things to say on monotheistic ideas, which helped to shape wider ideas in the West. Al-Fayyumi Saadiah Goan is another important philosopher who was particularly well-known for his translations and thoughts on Jewish law.

More recently, philosophers such as Yeshayahu Leibowitz have argued how important it is for Jews to observe their religion, even though this should not be mandated by the state or governments. He also wrote about the importance of Jewish people recognising the state of Israel. Emil Fackenheim, meanwhile, has been very influential in his arguments about the Holocaust and how important it is to keep Jewish ideas and tradition alive. He proposed doing this through the addition of a '614th commandment' to add to the 613 already included in the Torah.

Rabbinic Hermeneutics

Hermeneutics is a scary word, right? However, it's actually a pretty simple concept. It refers to biblical interpretation. In terms of rabbinic hermeneutics, it refers to the fact that as well as the Torah itself, many branches of Judaism – notably the Orthodox tradition – believe that the Torah also involves different interpretations of the scriptures.

Rabbis believed that the Torah had been communicated by God and that it was, therefore, consistent in its teachings. They used this as inspiration to look for deeper meanings within the text to provide more information as to how to interpret and apply the laws. There are different formulations of rabbinic hermeneutics:
- The 32 rules of R. Eliezer b. Yose ha-Gelili
- The 7 rules of Hillel
- The 13 rules of R. Ishmael

The rules of Hillel came before the rules of Ishmael, and the rules of Ishmael are generally thought to be an extension of those laid out by Hillel. This is why the 13 rules of Ishmael are most frequently referenced in rabbinic hermeneutics. These rules can be used by people who are studying the Torah, giving them a set of guidelines for when they are looking for new interpretations and other meanings within the text.

The rules can sometimes come across as a bit complicated, but there are some things that we can draw from them to get an idea of how hermeneutics works in the Jewish tradition.

For example, one of the laws states that if something is true in one situation, then it will also be true in another situation where similar circumstances exist. A good example of this is in Deuteronomy, which states that if a criminal is executed, the body should not be left out on the gallows overnight. An interpretation of this in hermeneutic terms is that since God handed down the scriptures of Deuteronomy, if he doesn't want to see the blood of a criminal, he would be even more distressed in the event of seeing the blood of an innocent. In this way, the same law applies to similar situations even though the contexts are different.

Another rule states that if something specific is singled out of a more general subject, that specific instance must also apply to the more general issue. An example of this is capital punishment. For instance, the punishment for divination by a ghost is death by stoning. This is the specific example. Since divination by a ghost is related to the wider issue of witchcraft, we can deduce that the punishment for other sins of witchcraft must also be death by stoning.

A modern (and slightly lighter) way of looking at this could be choosing what to eat and drink: someone might give you a list of options of what's available in their house (chips, biscuits, tea), providing you with specific examples – but there are more types of food and drink in the world than they have available at that particular time. In short, the specific and the general rely upon each other. This is just one example to show how specific examples can relate to more general, wider subjects. This is one of the key principles of rabbinic hermeneutics as discussed in the 13 rules of Ishmael.

Chapter 4: Jewish Observations

Jewish ethics

Ethics – the moral ideas that govern the behaviour of a group. With this definition in mind, it's pretty clear to see why morality plays such a crucial role in Jewish ethics, many of which have been around for thousands of years.

This involves not only the norms that have been established but also what are termed 'ways of the world' – *derekh eretz* in Hebrew. One of the unique things about Jewish ethics in this sense is the important role that God plays in the moral struggle of humanity. For example, God and prophecy are thought to be the keepers of morality, not man and wisdom as many other branches of ethics specify.

Jewish ethics are focused on eradicating injustice, and believe that cruelty and suffering can rock the foundation of a society. This can be seen, for instance, in the common Jewish attitude to capital punishment. Although this is not strictly prohibited by the Torah, study of the Talmud reveals that the rabbis who created this elaboration on the Torah's written principles made it so difficult to carry out the death penalty it is practically impossible to do so. This is reflected in practice in the state of Israel, where the death penalty has been abolished.

This also shows that Jewish ethics require that man cannot be complacent about morality; although the rules of the game might come from God, it is up to people on earth to carry them out. Ethics also apply to what's inside a person's head as well as the actions they carry out as it all falls under the sphere of morality. This can be seen in examples such as the commandment that warns against coveting thy neighbour's wife.

The relationship with animals is also an interesting part of Jewish ethics. Animals are seen as partners in the development of the world, although they are junior to mankind. This means that Jewish people believe that, like humans, animals should be allowed to rest on the Shabbat. They should be treated with compassion and people should not inflict pain on animals because they are also creatures of God. However, it can still be acceptable to kill an animal in order to fulfil a human need due to the fact that animals play the role of 'junior partner' (and, y'know, some of them taste good).

Even though people are allowed to kill animals for purposes such as food, clothing and parchment under Jewish law, there are still strict rules that need to be followed. For example, the Torah states that a person should feed their animals before feeding themselves and that a cow and her calf cannot be killed on the same day. Hunting is forbidden, and there are very strict rules on how animals can be used in research experiments.

The example of how Jewish people treat animals is a good way to demonstrate the key points of Jewish ethics. As well as morality, it is centred on compassion, kindness and respect for all creatures, while still acknowledging that mankind is the most important – this means that mankind has a responsibility to other creatures and needs to take very seriously how others are treated, no matter what their species.

Prayers

Just like prayers in all religions, the purpose of praying for Jewish people is to build the relationship between the individual and God. There are many different ways of praying, but this quote from Deuteronomy sums up one of the main reasons the act of praying is considered so important:

> …to love the Lord your God, and to serve him with all your heart and with all your soul.
> *Deuteronomy, 11:13*

There are two principles that need to be observed when praying as part of Judaism: the prayer needs to be true, meaning it should be from the heart (no telling lies to God!); and there should be nothing else in your mind at the time you are praying – your focus should be entirely on God.

Jewish people are supposed to pray three times a day: once in the morning, once in the afternoon and then again in the evening. The idea behind regular prayer is that it helps to ensure a person's relationship with God is growing all the time. Think of it like a garden: it needs maintenance to keep it in good condition and to improve it, just like a person's relationship with their religion needs maintenance. Alternatively, think of it like learning a musical instrument: you always get better with practice, making it more meaningful over time and the more you put into it (with any luck, anyway).

As well as praying three times a day, there are three different types of prayer in Judaism.
- A prayer of thanksgiving
- A prayer that asks God for something
- A prayer of praise

There is a theory in Judaism that was put forward by a rabbi, which suggests that the more a person asks God to help them – essentially, the more they pray – the more God will love them. Jewish people also believe that God listens to their prayers and that He always takes action, as a result.

> Interesting Fact: Whilst Hebrew is the most common language of Jewish prayer, Jews believe that God can understand them no matter what language they use. Even prayers sent up in silence can be understood.

The Shema is the most important prayer in Judaism. One interesting fact about the Shema is that it is not directed at God. Rather, it is directed at the Jewish people themselves. The prayer is written in the Torah, and it essentially tells the Israelites what their mission is. This includes loving God, accepting His teachings and passing them on to your children.

Also, a lot of Jewish prayers take place in the synagogue. This involves reading aloud the written services. As well as prayer, this is also about community and reaffirming the fact that you are part of the faith. This is not only important to the individual, but it also symbolises just how important the community is to Judaism.

The Jewish prayer book is called a siddur. It includes writings from across the centuries, charting different aspects and periods of Judaism. As well as writings from important Jewish thinkers, it also includes poetry written in Hebrew. The prayers often include lessons and thoughts to reflect on, as well as prayers that can be spoken to God.

Giving a blessing is another form of Jewish prayer, and this usually happens before sitting down to a meal or before important events. This is to acknowledge the hand of God in everything and gives thanks for what God has imparted to mankind.

Religious clothing

Fashion is always so complicated, isn't it? You can't wear this, those colours clash, don't wear that fabric, that dress makes you look like a potato with legs… And the religious rules of Judaism make things even more complicated.

First of all, the Torah prohibits wool and flax from being worn. Specifically, in Deuteronomy, it says 'You shall not wear combined fibres, wool and linen together.' The forbidden type of fabric is called shatnez. Deuteronomy also states that men and women should not wear each other's clothes in order to help maintain the distinctness between the sexes.

Judaism also has some teachings on head coverings: for example, there is a story about a young man who was destined to be a thief. He was told to cover his head so that he would always retain his fear of heaven. Now, many Jews wear a skullcap called a kippah as a symbol of their religiousness, and it is considered by some to be a requirement of Torah law (this is disputed by others).

Another type of Jewish religious clothing is the tzitzit, which is a form of tassel that is often worn by men and women during prayer. The wearing of tzitzis helps to remind Jews that they are servants of the Lord. This is because there are five knots on each tassel to represent the first five books of the Torah.

Torah readings

Public Torah readings play an important role in Judaism, and the practice of reading the Torah aloud can be dated back as far as Moses. However, it was a man named Ezra the Scribe who first started the current tradition of Torah readings, giving set days on which parts of the Torah should be read.

This involves reading the Torah in the morning on Mondays and Thursdays, and reading it in the afternoons on the Shabbat. This calendar was put into place so that people would never go for more than three days without a Torah reading. Also, Mondays and Thursdays were originally chosen for Torah readings because that was when Jewish people went into town to shop. The phrase 'killing two birds with one stone' springs to mind.

Public Torah readings have been going on without interruption since 2CE – an impressive record! Also, the Torah is read in sequence. There are different ways of splitting it up in order to be read. For example, it originally took three years to read when it was split into 155 sections in Israel. Some movements of Judaism, such as Reform and some Conservative Jews, stick to this cycle to the current day.

However, other movements of Judaism split the Torah into different sections. Most Conservative Jews and all Orthodox Jews follow the pattern that was set up in Babylonia. The cycle lasts for a year and splits the Torah into 54 sections.

When the Torah is read at the synagogue, there are always at least three people involved to represent the fact that God worked through an intermediary when passing on his message. The Torah also has to be read in a particular way, so the role of one of the people involved is to correct the pronunciation of the reader where necessary. While it is being read, the Torah scroll cannot be touched; instead, a long silver 'hand' is used to track the progress of the reader instead.

Synagogues and religious buildings

The synagogue is where Jewish people go to worship, to listen to services and to pray to God. The word 'synagogue' is actually Greek, and it means 'meeting place' or somewhere to come together – which is exactly the purpose it serves in Judaism. They are sometimes also referred to as temples, particularly by Reform Jews.

> Interesting Fact: There are no altars in synagogues. This is because altars are associated with sacrifice, and the only place Jews are allowed to make a sacrifice is the temple built by Solomon in Jerusalem.

The temple built by Solomon in Jerusalem was destroyed by the Babylonians but then rebuilt when the Persians took over. However, it was destroyed again in 70AD when the First Jewish Revolt was crushed by Titus. Since then, the temple has not been rebuilt, and Jews have not made any sacrifices to their God.

The concept of the synagogue is thought to have begun with exactly what the word means – somewhere for people to come together. This didn't necessarily have to be a formal religious place and could even have been somewhere simple like someone's living room (and for many today, we're sure the living room – the sofa and television in particular – is still something close to a religious experience). However, synagogues soon became very important to Judaism, and there are plenty of ancient examples of places of religious worship, such as one built in Syria in around 200AD and one in Cordoba, in Spain.

> Interesting Fact: In order for a proper service to be conducted in a synagogue, a quorum (a minyan) needs to be achieved or else the Torah will not be read from the scroll. This means that at least 10 adults need to be in attendance.

Typically, there are three services a day at a synagogue, along with special services for holy days. A service usually involves public prayers, a blessing, private prayers and concluding prayers. Other events such as weddings, funerals, meetings and study classes can also take place there.

There are also other buildings that hold a religious significance for Jewish people. For example, the mikvah is a sort of bathhouse that is typically used by Orthodox Jews on special occasions, such as before the Sabbath. Orthodox Jews also make use of buildings called yeshivas. This is a type of school or seminary for Orthodox Jews and acts as a place where they can undertake advanced study of the Talmud.

Dietary laws: kashrut

Kashrut is a word that refers to the Jewish dietary laws, and it governs what Jews are able to eat, as well as how they must prepare and eat food. The more common word for this that you have probably heard of is 'kosher'. However, while kashrut refers to the dietary laws, kosher refers to food that is made in accordance with those laws. 'Treif' is the word that is normally used to describe food that isn't kosher.

One of the reasons kashrut first developed was due to health; it helped to keep Jewish people healthy at a time when food preparation was nowhere near as safe as it is today. However, this is not the only reason. Some of the rules came about because of practicalities. For example, hundreds of years ago, it was more useful to use a camel as transport than to eat it.

Kashrut rules include:
- Pigs, camels, rock badgers and hares cannot be eaten.
- Shellfish cannot be eaten.
- Meat cannot be eaten with dairy.
- Grape products (like wine) made by people who are not Jewish cannot be eaten.
- Utensils used with meat cannot then be used with dairy.
- Kosher practices must be maintained
- The Torah prohibits the consumption of blood

Laws of ritual purity

The laws of ritual purity are another important aspect of Judaism. They relate to issues of being unclean, which is thought to occur due to seminal or vaginal flux and menstruation amongst other things. The rules also relate to coming into contact with human corpses or graves, which will be used as an example here.

It is important to note that the rules of ritual purity are not as vital as they once were because they largely applied to the temple of sacrifice, built by Solomon in Jerusalem and discussed elsewhere in this guide. This means they are not as applicable today as they once were, but the concepts of tumah and taharah (uncleanliness and cleanliness) are still important in Jewish tradition.

A man or a woman who is considered to be spiritually impure, such as because they have come into contact with a corpse, was not allowed to enter the House of God. They were also not allowed to eat the sacrificial parts of the sacrificed animal due to their impurity. The reason they were not allowed to enter the synagogue was because the role of the holy building is to build the relationship between them and God; this cannot be achieved whilst impure.

Family Purity

Ahem. Now we come to 'the sex bit,' otherwise known as 'family purity'. In Judaism, this largely revolves around the concept of Niddah. This is sometimes known as the laws of separation, and it concerns the husband and wife staying apart whilst the woman is menstruating. It is mainly Orthodox Jewish communities that take part in Niddah, with more liberal Jewish movements not observing it at all.

Essentially, the Torah forbids a man from having sex with a woman who is menstruating. This is linked to the laws of ritual purity, with menstruation being seen as unclean in a way. Interestingly, Niddah is the only part of ritual purity that continues until this day. After the destruction of the Jerusalem temple in 70CE, the rest of the laws have fallen by the wayside.

The separation between the man and woman has to last for a minimum of 12 days. The rabbis also extended the rules laid out in the Torah; while the Torah only prohibits sexual intercourse, the rabbis also decided that a man should not even touch his wife or sleep in the same bed as her during the separation period. This means that Orthodox Jews have to be particularly careful when organising weddings to make sure the woman is not in Niddah at the time.

Life-cycle events

Let's go for a quick dash through the most important events in a Jewish person's life.

The first of these is the B'rit Milah. This is the circumcision ceremony that is performed on baby boys when they are eight days old. This has to be carried out by a trained rabbi and only men can be present when the circumcision happens. A male relative has to hold the child during the circumcision, after which the baby's name will be announced.

The Bar Mitzvah is the next significant life-cycle event in Judaism. This generally happens when a boy is 13 years old, and the preparation for the ceremony is usually taken very seriously. On the Sabbath after his 13th birthday, the boy will be called up at the synagogue to read from the Torah. This marks his entrance into the adult community. For girls, the ceremony happens when they are 12, and it usually involves a group of girls going through the process together. However, girls only get to read from the Torah in Reform and Liberal Judaism, which place less emphasis on the differences between men and women.

Kiddushin, or marriage, is the next major life event. The bride stands to the right of the groom and then the ceremony takes place under a canopy called a huppah. They take their vows and drink from a goblet. The rabbi also reads out a contract, detailing the responsibilities of the husband to his wife.

Death is the final life cycle event. The dead are always buried. Ideally, the body needs to be buried within 24 hours, a service will be held and a tribute given. There is then a seven day period of mourning. However, Jewish people believe that death is not really the end, and that they will be resurrected at the Day of Judgement.

Chapter 5: Jewish Holidays

The Jewish comedian and violinist Henny Youngman once said 'I once wanted to become an atheist but I gave up… they have no holidays.' This brings us nicely onto the exciting bit – the great range of Jewish holidays!

Shabbat

In Judaism, Shabbat is the day of rest, otherwise known as the Sabbath. This takes place every week from the time the sun goes down on Friday until the nightfall on Saturday. Since it is the day of rest, very little is allowed to be done on the Shabbat, which means much of the preparation for it – such as cooking – has to be done in advance. We imagine lots of Jewish households end up eating Chinese takeout if they forget to prepare the stuff in advance…

The lady of the household is required to light two candles 18 minutes before the sun goes down on the Friday. She also has to recite a blessing while covering her eyes. Later in the evening, if possible at the synagogue, there will be a special Friday evening prayer ceremony. This is followed by a festive meal.

This meal begins with a Kiddush blessing, which should be done using grape juice or wine. The glass is held in the right hand, the blessing is recited, and then the wine or grape juice is drunk. After the Kiddush and before the meal starts properly, everyone needs to wash their hands and say another blessing before drying their hands. Following this, the head of the household will break into two loaves of bread, say another blessing and then hand around the pieces of bread so that the meal can begin.

There are more prayers on Shabbat morning, followed by the main day of rest.

Three pilgrimage festivals

There are three festivals in the Jewish calendar that used to require male Israelites to make the pilgrimage to Jerusalem and offer a sacrifice at the temple.

One of these festivals is Passover, which has been celebrated since around 1300BCE. You can read the story of Passover in Exodus. The purpose of this particular festival is to celebrate Moses leading all of the Jews out of Egypt. In the modern day, the Passover festival lasts for seven or eight days. In preparation, the house must be thoroughly cleaned, and the festival involves ritual meals with specific food that has symbolic value.

The second of the three pilgrimage festivals is Shavuot. This is a harvest festival that was traditionally held to mark the end of the barley harvest and the start of the wheat harvest. It is also held in remembrance of when the Jews were given the Torah at Mount Sinai, which we have already looked at elsewhere in this guide.

The third festival is Sukkot. This is held to remember all the time the Jews spent in the desert while they were on their way to the Promised Land. It is also to mark the protection that God gave them during that time and celebrations often include spending time in a hut in the garden with a hole in the roof so that they are protected by God in heaven.

High holy days

Throughout the year, there are several high holy days that are observed by Jewish people.

The first of these is Rosh Hashanah, which marks the start of the Jewish New Year, the date of which can vary. This lasts for two days, and it is also thought to be a time of judgement when God weighs up the good things against the bad things a person has done over the past year.

Next up is Yom Kippur, which is the Day of Atonement and takes place soon after Rosh Hashanah. Yom Kippur is the most sacred day of the year, and it follows the Days of Repentance. It is when God decides the fate of a person for the next year. We bet everyone's on their best behaviour on this day.

Sukkot, the Feast of Tabernacles, is the next High Holy Day. As discussed above, this is when the Jews remember the time spent in the desert and huts are often built for the purpose.

Then there is Hanukkah. This is the festival of lights, and it lasts for eight days. It is usually celebrated in November or December. The festival is to celebrate the triumph of the Maccabee Jews over the Syrian Greek army.

Finally, there is Purim. This festival celebrates a woman called Esther, who saved from extermination a group of Jews living in Persia. The festival involves a reading from the Book of Esther, as well as a carnival, which makes it a popular Jewish holiday.

Purim

As mentioned briefly above, the festival of Purim is to celebrate the triumph of Esther when she saved the Jews in Syria. The villain of the piece is called Haman and, during the Purim synagogue service, every time his name is mentioned, he is booed like a pantomime villain.

Purim is generally considered to be one of the most fun Jewish holy days. The main religious element of the day is that the Book of Esther is read aloud. This happens on the evening before Purim and on the day of Purim itself. There are usually also lots of carnival-like celebrations, with many people dressing up to go to the synagogue. Children often dress up as characters from the story of Esther.

The festival is celebrated in the twelfth month of the Jewish calendar, which is usually in March. The word 'Purim' means 'lots'. This is a reference to the lottery used by Haman when he was trying to decide what date to exterminate the Jews on before Esther saved them.

There is a brief period of fasting prior to the festival, but during Purim itself, there is lots of eating and drinking. Charity donations are also encouraged, either in the form of money or as gifts.

Hanukkah

Lasting for eight days, Hanukkah is the Jewish Festival of Light. It is two hundred years older than Christianity, meaning that it is very long-lived.

The festival is celebrated to commemorate the three-year war that took place between the Maccabee Jews and the Syrian Greek army. This was said to be the most powerful army in the world at the time, and it took a huge amount of effort for the Maccabees to recapture the city of Jerusalem and their temple.

When they rededicated the temple, they found inside it a small amount of oil, still sealed. They needed it to light their menorah, which has 8 branches on it. Unfortunately, there was only enough oil for one day.

However, miraculously, the oil ended up burning for 8 whole days. This is why the menorah is still lit during the modern Hanukkah festival. One branch is lit per day, moving from right to left. Jews say additional blessings on top of their ordinary prayers during Hanukkah. This happens just before the candles are lit. Hymns are also sung.

Hanukkah is also known for its food, particularly fried food, as this is reminiscent of the oil miracle (sounds yummy, too). Games are also played during the festival, and it is customary to give gifts.

Other holidays

Tisha B'av takes place on the 9th day of the Jewish month of Av. This is a time when the Jewish people remember the tragedies that have befallen them over the centuries, including the destruction of their temples. It is a solemn affair, associated with prayers and fasting, and is a time of mourning.

Yom Hashoah is a recent Jewish holiday. It is a day where they remember the Holocaust. It was established in 1959 in Israel. Again, this is very solemn, and memorial prayers are said for the people who died in the Holocaust.

Tu B'Shevat is one of the four Jewish New Years. Specifically, it is the New Year for trees and Jews eat fruit mentioned in the Torah to mark the occasion.

Chapter 6: Other Religion

Influence on Christianity

Judaism has had a highly significant influence on Christianity; as we have already discussed, Christianity is a religion that came out of Judaism, meaning that the two religions are linked. Also, even though they are significantly different, Judaism has influenced large aspects of Christianity.

For example, the two religions share part of their holy books: the full version of the Jewish Written Torah is the Old Testament of the Christian bible. Where they differ is that Jewish people believe the Old Testament is all they need for their religion whereas Christians believe they also need the New Testament to be able to make proper sense of it.

Also, when Christianity first came into being, there were very strong Jewish influences at work. In fact, the original Christian church was influenced by two main parties: the Gentile party and the Judaizing party, which worked to promote the continuance of the Jewish religion. For a time, the Judaizing party had a big impact on the Gentile faction, requiring them to continue with Jewish practices even as the new religion developed.

However, over time the influence of the Judaizing party waned, and it was decided that Christians who were born Jews didn't need to continue in the law of Moses, and that Gentile Christians no longer needed to observe Jewish practices either. This led to the need for new services and texts to replace the old Jewish ones, as well as new practices for worship. This led to the development of the New Testament, new priesthoods and other new practices.

Another influence that Judaism has had on Christianity is in its belief in only one God. As we have seen in the History section of this guide, the idea of believing in a single God started with Abraham, one of the Jewish patriarchs. This has continued with Christianity. However, one of the main ways in which the religions differ is in the Christian worship of Jesus. While Jews believe that God can never have a corporeal form, Christians worship Jesus as God's son, which helps to show how the religions began to diverge as the centuries passed.

Also, both Judaism and Christianity have a belief that the Messiah will one day appear. Where they differ is that Christians believe he has already come once in Jesus, whereas Jews believe the Messianic era has yet to arrive at all. Jews, therefore, believe that Jesus was an ordinary man, however, given the fact that he and his disciples were all Jewish prior to the founding of Christianity, it is possible to see further influences of Judaism on the Christian religion.

Both Christians and Jews believe in the 10 commandments given in the Old Testament. The difference is that those 10 commandments are the only ones Christians subscribe to; Jews believe that there are 613 commandments in the Torah in total. They also share a belief that the prophets in the bible are true prophets.

Even though the relations between Christianity and Judaism have often been strained over the years, today there is a greater understanding between them – and it is hard to deny the impact that Judaism has had on Christianity, not least in helping to give it life in the first place.

Influence on Islam

One of the main ways Judaism and Islam are linked is through Abraham; both religions see him as an important part of the history of their respective faiths. However, while Abraham is seen in some ways as a father of Judaism, for Muslims it was his son Ishmael who is seen as the father of the Arab people. Despite this slight difference, Abraham is still vital to both faiths and is seen as the root of the religions.

There are many other similarities between the religions that allow us to see the influence of Christianity on Islam. For example, both faiths circumcise their baby boys according to Abrahamic law. They are both also of Semitic origin and both worship only one God, thanks to Abraham's discovery of monotheism.

Both faiths also see Jerusalem as their holy city and the Temple Mount, where Abraham took his son to sacrifice him to God, is also important to both religions. Another way in which their influence can be seen in each other is in the fact that has well as having written scriptures, they both also share oral traditions that are just as important – if not more, in some cases.

Shared religious concepts can also be found between Judaism and Islam. For example, they both believe in a coming day of Divine Judgement and they both believe in an afterlife of some sort. They both also believe that studying religious law is a form of worship and they both take this seriously in their respective religions. They both also are required to fast from time to time, have a belief in charity, and many of their ritual purity and dietary laws are very similar. For example, pork is not allowed in either religion.

All of this shows just how similar Judaism and Islam are. Since Judaism was created centuries before Islam, which originated around 7CE, we can see just how much of an influence it has had on the religion. They are often referred to as the two religions that have the most in common with each other since so many of their practices and beliefs overlap. Once Islam began to take hold and develop in the Middle East – the same area where Judaism came into being – it also started to have an influence on Judaism, and this tradition of influencing each other has continued throughout the subsequent centuries.

Probably the main way in which the religions differ is in the Islamic worship of the prophet Mohammed. They believe that he was the last and greatest prophet, whereas Jewish people believe that Moses was the greatest prophet of them all. However, they both believe that their written laws (the Written Torah and the Quran) were sent by God and that they are essentially perfect. These books are very different in their form, though, highlighting the fact that differences between the religions do exist.

Overall, Judaism has had a significant influence on Islam, which we can see in the fact much of the religions are so similar. However, they are also extremely distinct, and we cannot deny the fact they these are two separate traditions in their own right.

Conclusion

Through this book, we have looked at a range of aspects relating to Judaism. We've gone on a journey through its history, beliefs, customs and practices, and its influences on other religions. We've seen that even though Judaism has at times been troubled – and at others cruelly persecuted – it has always endured.

Let's finish with a quote from the actress Janet Suzman, who once said of Judaism: 'I find its attention to living this life rather than the next one exhilarating because I think even independently of Judaism that that's the right way to go about life.'

That sounds about right, doesn't it?

About the Publisher

BookCaps™ is building a library of low cost study guides; if you enjoyed this book, look for other books in the "Plain and Simple English" series at **www.bookcaps.com**.

Manufactured by Amazon.ca
Bolton, ON